THE NATURE COMPANY
Naturalist's Journal

NATURE TRAVEL

*Mountains complement desert
as desert complements city,
as wilderness complements and
completes civilization.*

Desert Solitaire,
EDWARD ABBEY (1927–89),
American writer

Something will have gone out of us as a people if we ever let the remaining wilderness be destroyed... if we pollute the last clean air and dirty the last clean streams and push our paved roads through the last of the silence.

WALLACE STEGNER (1909–93),
American writer

A man who concerns himself principally with the artificial, and who thinks that the world is for... business alone, misses entirely the divine halo that rest about much in nature.

Days Afield on Staten Island,
WILLIAM T. DAVIS (1862–1945),
American businessman, naturalist, and
amateur entomologist

Traveler's Notes

The whooping crane stands 5 feet (1.5 m) tall, with a wingspan of 7 feet (2.2 m). A very well-known North American endangered bird, it is being rescued from the brink of extinction by imaginative programs such as one begun in Idaho in 1976, in which whooping crane eggs were placed in sand-hill crane nests. Every year the population of around 165 cranes makes the long winter migration to the Aransas National Wildlife Refuge on the Gulf Coast of Texas. Their breeding range is in the swampy conifer country of Wood Buffalo National Park, Canada.

Ah to be alive
on a mid-September morn
fording a stream
barefoot, pants rolled up,
holding boots, pack on,
sunshine, ice in the shallows,
northern rockies.

For All,
GARY SNYDER (b. 1930),
American poet

Traveler's Notes

North America's largest toad, the giant toad, grows up to 6 inches (15 cm) in length. It is found in a very limited range around the Rio Grande Valley of Texas and in parts of South Florida. It lays thousands of eggs, but few of its young reach maturity because, despite highly toxic secretions on their skin that make them taste unpleasant, they are eaten by a number of predators. Those that do reach adulthood return to the pond of their birth to breed, guided by a strong homing instinct and the sound of the chorus from their particular pond.

*How strange and wonderful is our home,
our earth with its swirling vaporous
atmosphere, its flowing and frozen
liquids, its trembling plants,
its creeping, crawling, climbing
creatures... the furry grass,
the scaly seas.*

EDWARD ABBEY (1927–89),
American writer

Are you aware of the beautiful sunset
and the clean, salt smell of the sea?

The Winner's Notebook,
THEODORE ISAAC RUBIN (b. 1923),
American psychiatrist and writer

The gray seal is a large mammal, with adult males growing to more than 12 feet (4 m) in length. It is found on both sides of the Atlantic, and as far south as Maine. The gray seal, like other seals, cannot turn its hind flippers forward and must haul itself across land by means of its fore flippers when it comes ashore to bask or whelp. The pups of this species are born during summer with a warm, cream, woolly coat, which is replaced within about three weeks with a short-haired, blue-gray, sea-going one.

A clear breeze has no price,
The bright moon no owner.

Song Hon (1535–98),
Korean poet

One of North America's most
handsome waterfowl, the wood
duck frequents the wooded swamps
and streams of North America. The
female is more muted in color than
the flamboyant green and purple
crested male. Unlike other ducks,
this species is seldom seen in flocks,
although strongly bonded pairs
stay together to live and travel, even
outside the nesting season.

A wonderful place to see them is
Erie National Wildlife Refuge in
Pennsylvania, where some 20
species of duck are regular visitors.

...Breezes of the South!
Who toss the golden and the flame-like flowers,
And pass the prairie-hawk that, poised on high,
Flaps his broad wings, yet moves not.

The Prairies,
WILLIAM CULLEN BRYANT (1754–1812),
American poet, critic, and editor

*[Nature] is the one place where miracles not only
happen, but happen all the time.*

THOMAS WOLFE (1900–38),
American novelist

Remaining virtually unchanged for nearly 200 million years, horseshoe crabs have survived all their close relatives. They are an unmistakable sight from the Gulf Coast of Maine to the Gulf Coast of Mexico. They run along the sea floor with a curious bobbing gait, eating baby clams, dead fish, and marine worms. In spring, horseshoe crabs come ashore in their millions to spawn along the Atlantic coast, attracting countless shore birds that feast on their eggs. Each female lays 200–300 eggs, which hatch about six weeks later.

Despite sharp-tailed grouse being
among the strongest flyers of all the
grouse, they prefer to remain on
the ground. They can be found in
a variety of habitats, from prairies
and cleared areas, to thickets, bogs,
and brushlands, throughout Alaska,
Canada, Colorado, and Washington.
During winter, sharp-tails take to
the trees to feed on buds and only
return to their earthbound way of
life when spring arrives with berries
and flowers for foraging.

There was an Old Man with a beard,
Who said, "It is just as I feared!—
Two Owls and a Hen,
Four Larks and a Wren,
Have all built their nests in my beard!"

There was an Old Man with a Beard,
EDWARD LEAR (1812–88),
English writer of comic nonsense

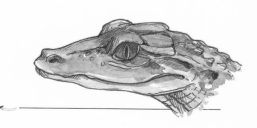

I travel not to go anywhere, but to go.
I travel for travel's sake.
The great affair is to move.

Travels with a Donkey,
ROBERT LOUIS STEVENSON (1850–94),
Scottish poet, writer, and essayist

Pale green, with a yellow head and black neck rings, the collared lizard grows to about a foot (30 cm) in length and is found throughout the midwest and southwest regions of North America. It is wary, sure-footed, and fast-moving, propelling its body forward with strong back legs. Although difficult to capture, if confined it will inflict a nasty bite. In desert areas, it lives mainly on spiders and insects. Like other reptiles, it has adapted to reduce the loss of water from its body by having no glands on its skin through which it can be excreted.

*...He had done this thing before, somewhere in
that other and dimly remembered world,
and he was doing it again, now, running
free in the open, the unpacked earth
underfoot, the wide sky overhead.*

The Call of the Wild,
JACK LONDON (1876–1916),
American novelist

Gray wolves are especially sensitive to the intrusion of humans, so roam only over the remote parts of Canada, Alaska, the US area around the Great Lakes, and the Rockies. The pack takes the lead of the strongest male when hunting. The animals often follow in each other's tracks, making a single line in the snow. They mostly feed on caribou and moose, usually killing the weaker, older, or infirm, thereby completing the natural and necessary cycle of life in the wild.

The red wolf, once hunted almost to extinction, is being returned to the wild through captive breeding.

Akela, the great gray Lone Wolf who led all the Pack by strength and cunning, lay out at full length on his rock, and below him sat forty or more wolves of every size and color, from badger-colored veterans who could handle a buck alone, to young black three-year-olds who thought they could.

The Jungle Book,
RUDYARD KIPLING (1865–1936),
English novelist, poet, and
short-story writer

The lady's slipper orchid is a deciduous terrestrial plant that prefers cold, partly shady, and boggy conditions. The leaves are elliptical and the pretty flowers have a pouch-like lip petal that looks rather like a moccasin or Dutch clog. Many species of lady's slipper orchid have been removed from their original habitat, so much so that they have become a rarity in the wild. Uprooting or picking wildflowers for transplanting in an ornamental garden setting is not only ecologically unsound, it is also futile, as they almost always perish outside of their native setting.

How Love burns through the Putting in the Seed
On through the watching for that early birth
When, just as the soil tarnishes with weed,
The sturdy seedling with arched body comes
Shouldering its way and shedding the earth crumbs.

Putting in the Seed,
ROBERT FROST (1874–1963),
American poet

Consuming up to 100 pounds
(45 kg) of plant material a day, the
manatee is valued by humans for
the assistance this gives in keeping
our waterways clear.

The manatee is a docile aquatic
mammal, sleeping and giving birth
in river estuaries and shallow coastal
waters of the southeastern US.
It uses its pointed fore-paddles and
broad, spoon-shaped tail to propel
itself gently through the water. The
fragile population of about 2,000 is
constantly threatened by water craft
collisions, along with toxicosis,
caused by the red tide—proliferating
red-colored microorganisms.

The sea, once it casts its spell,
holds one in its net of wonder forever.

Jacques-Yves Cousteau (b. 1910),
French conservationist and marine explorer

*Panting and snorting like a mad battle
steed that has lost its rider, the
masterless ocean overruns the globe.*

Moby-Dick,
HERMAN MELVILLE (1819–91),
American novelist and poet

Unlike other spoonbills, which are all white, the roseate spoonbill is partly pink with deeper pink and vivid carmine feathers on its wings. Now fully protected after being on the verge of extinction, it is found in salt marshes, mangrove swamps, and freshwater lagoons along the Gulf Coast of Florida and Texas. This spectacular wader stands up to 31 inches (80 cm) tall, and feeds by sweeping its characteristic spoon-shaped bill back and forth through the water, straining out small fish and crustaceans for nourishment.

Thousands of tired, nerve-shaken, over-civilized
people are beginning to find out that going
to the mountains is going home; that
wilderness is a necessity...

Our National Parks,
JOHN MUIR (1838–1914),
Scottish-born American naturalist and writer

*Sunsets and rainbows, green forest and restive blue
seas, all naturally colored things are my siblings.
We have played together on the floor
of the world since the first stone
looked up at the stars.*

MAYA ANGELOU (b. 1928),
American writer

The country lay bare and entirely leafless around him, and he thought that he had never seen so far and so intimately into the insides of things as on that winter day when Nature was deep in her annual slumber and seemed to have kicked the clothes off.

The Wind in the Willows,
KENNETH GRAHAME (1859–1932),
English novelist

~✕~

The North American grizzly bear ranges in color from light fawn to deep reddish brown and can weigh up to 1,100 pounds (500 kg). Grizzy bears, like most other bears, have the instinct to hibernate during the bleak winter months, to ensure survival. They do this by establishing a den in readiness.

Although classed as carnivores, grizzlies relish eating roots, leaves, fruits, and berries. They also commonly make a meal of salmon, using their sharp claws and teeth to fish them out of streams.

And through the wintry months so pale
The sumach's brilliant hues recall;
Where, waving over hill and vale,
They gave its splendor to our fall.

The Sumach Leaves,
JONES VERY (1813–80),
American poet

All Nature was wide awake and stirring now,
long lances of sunlight pierced down through
the dense foliage far and near, and a few
butterflies came fluttering upon the scene.

Tom Sawyer,
MARK TWAIN (1835–1910),
American writer and humorist

Traveler's Notes

The Olympic marmot only
inhabits the Olympic Mountains,
Washington. It is a close relative
of the hoary marmot, and is often
regarded as a subspecies of that
mammal. The marmot lives in
burrows 9–15 inches (23–38 cm)
deep. It hibernates during winter,
relying on its body fat stores for
sustenance. The Olympic marmot's
rocky surroundings provide it with
a necessary escape route from
carnivorous predators. Even though
the underground burrow may be
relatively safe, it doesn't stop larger
mammals, such as bears, from
digging it up in search of a meal.

Flying? I've been to almost as many places as my luggage.

BOB HOPE (b. 1903),
American actor and comedian

Although extremely graceful both on the water and in flight, the American white pelican has some difficulty becoming airborne due to its size. It has a wingspan of up to 9 feet (3 m), and to get sufficient lift, it must "run" along the surface of the water. It breeds in summer, in large colonies in the west of the US, and then makes a spectacular migration to marshes and lagoons of the Southeast and Mexico for the winter. During the breeding season, a horn-like growth appears on the bill of both sexes, but is shed after the eggs are laid.

The earth spirit has been layed down
It is covered over with growing things,
It has been laid down
The earth is beautiful

NAVAJO CHANT

Those who contemplate the beauty of the earth find reserves of strength that will endure as long as life lasts.

The Sense of Wonder,
RACHEL CARSON (1907–64),
American naturalist and writer

These are the gardens of the desert, these
The unshorn fields, boundless and beautiful,
For which the speech of England has no name—
The Prairies. I behold them for the first,
And my heart swells.

The Prairies,
WILLIAM CULLEN BRYANT (1754–1812),
American poet, critic, and editor

...all who have achieved real excellence in any art, possess one thing in common, that is, a mind to obey nature, to be one with nature, throughout the four seasons of the year.

BASHO (1644–94),
Japanese poet and diarist

The sidewinder snake is found in windblown desert areas of the southwestern US and northern Mexico. It is a poisonous rattlesnake, only measuring about 27 inches (70 cm). It is sandy brown, or yellowish, and sometimes even a pinkish color. The sidewinder uses a method of locomotion known as "sidewinding", which is highly effective over loose sand. It involves lifting the entire body, leaving only two points in contact with the ground—the head and tail tip. This is also an efficient method of controlling body temperature by limiting contact with the sand.

When an oak tree is felled, the whole forest echoes with it, but a hundred acorns are planted silently by some unseen force.

THOMAS CARLYLE (1795–1881),
Scottish-born English prose writer

The loggerhead turtle is the second largest of the sea turtles, about half the size of the largest, the leatherback, which grows to 8 feet (2.5 m). The turtle uses its powerful front flippers to swim very long distances and is found mainly in warm tropical seas. The loggerhead turtle, as with other sea turtles, is endangered. It comes ashore at night between April and August to lay around 100 eggs in a nest dug about 18 inches (45 cm) deep in the sand. By morning, the female loggerhead is back within the safety of the sea, leaving the eggs to hatch without further help from her or the male parent.

The waving of the boughs in the storm is new to me and old. It takes me by surprise, and yet is not unknown. Its effect is like that of a higher thought or a better emotion coming over me...

"Nature" from *Selected Essays,*
RALPH WALDO EMERSON (1803–82),
American poet, essayist, and philosopher

In many countries you remember your meals,
while in other—and I think more interesting—
places, you remember your illnesses.

PAUL THEROUX (b. 1941),
American writer

If you're lucky, you may see puffins nesting in colonies in the crevices of rocky cliffs and on grass-covered islets in remote parts of the West Coast and the northern Atlantic.

The horned puffin is one of the most populous species of bird to be found along the coast of Alaska. It is named after the small, fleshy appendage over each eye, which it raises or lowers at will. During the breeding season, distinctive colored growths appear on the male's beak, giving it a parrot-like appearance. The puffin's triangular, flattened bill is useful for catching and holding three or four small fish at a time.

There is not a sprig of grass that shoots uninteresting to me.

THOMAS JEFFERSON (1743–1826),
United States President

*In God's wilderness is the hope of the world—
the great fresh, unblighted, unredeemed
wilderness.*

JOHN MUIR (1849–1914),
Scottish-born American naturalist and writer

The forests within Shenandoah National Park, Virginia, were once thick with American chestnut trees which, because of the usefulness and beauty of the timber, were widely used for furniture, railroad ties, and tannin compounds.

In the early 1900s, however, a fungus was introduced, without intent, that has killed nearly all of these fine and valuable trees. Even when sprouts appear from their stumps, the fungus again manages to kill them. Such disasters underline the need for stringent protective measures to maintain healthy ecosystems throughout our land.

One touch of nature makes the
whole world kin.

WILLIAM SHAKESPEARE (1564–1616),
English playwright and poet

On the ragged edge of the world
I'll roam.
And the home of the wolf
Will be my home.

Robert N. Service (1874–1958),
English-born Canadian writer

TOP TRAVEL SPOTS IN NORTH AMERICA

Whether you want to explore old-growth forests, climb mountains, or wander beside the sea, there are numerous places to choose from when planning your travels.

Below are listed some of the most enriching and extraordinary locations in North America, each one supporting a fascinating array of flora and fauna. National parks and preserves offer the responsible traveler the challenges and rewards of activities such as birding, rock hounding, rafting, scuba diving, cross-country skiing, and hiking. Take a bike, a boat, or a horse. Whatever your interest and your favorite type of landscape, there's a destination waiting.

Top Forest Areas
Tongass National Forest, Alaska
Kings Canyon and Sequoia National Parks, California
Redwood National Park, California
Olympic National Park, Washington
Yellowstone National Park, Wyoming
Coronado National Forest, Arizona
Great Smoky Mountains National Park,
North Carolina and Tennessee

Top Mountain Areas
Denali National Park and Preserve, Alaska
Gates of the Arctic National Park and Preserve, Alaska
Yosemite National Park, California
Mount Rainier National Park, Washington
Rocky Mountain National Park, Colorado
Glacier National Park, Montana
White Mountain National Forest, New Hampshire
Banff National Park, Alberta

Top Grassland Areas
Bosque del Apache National Wildlife Refuge, New Mexico
Theodore Roosevelt National Park, North Dakota
The Tallgrass Prairie Preserve, Oklahoma
Wichita Mountains National Wildlife
Refuge, Oklahoma

Top Desert Areas
Death Valley National Park, California
Canyonlands National Park, Utah
Zion National Park, Utah
Grand Canyon National Park, Arizona
Saguaro National Monument, Arizona
Big Bend National Park, Texas

Top Wetland Areas
Kauai Refuge Complex, Hawaii
Medicine Lake National Wildlife Refuge, Montana
Bosque del Apache National Wildlife Refuge, New Mexico
Santa Ana/Lower Rio Grande Valley National Wildlife Refuges, Texas
Everglades National Park, Florida
Edwin B. Forsythe National Wildlife Refuge, New Jersey
Iroquois National Wildlife Refuge, New York

Top Coastal Areas
Point Reyes National Seashore, California
Olympic National Park, Washington
John Pennekamp Coral Reef State Park, Florida
Padre Island National Seashore, Texas
Acadia National Park, Maine
Gwaii Haanas National Park Reserve, British Columbia
Fundy National Park, New Brunswick

The Nature Company Naturalist's Journals are published by Time-Life Books

Conceived and produced by Weldon Owen Pty Limited
43 Victoria Street, McMahons Point, NSW, 2060, Australia
A member of the Weldon Owen Group of Companies
Sydney • San Francisco
Copyright 1997 © US Weldon Owen Inc.
Copyright 1997 © Weldon Owen Pty Ltd

THE NATURE COMPANY
Priscilla Wrubel, Ed Strobin, Steve Manning,
Georganne Papac, Tracy Fortini, Deanna Pervis

TIME-LIFE BOOKS
Time-Life Books is a division of Time Life Inc.
Time-Life is a trademark of Time Warner Inc. U.S.A.

Time-Life Custom Publishing
Vice-President and Publisher: Terry Newell
Director of New Product Development: Regina Hall
Managing Editor: Donia Ann Steele
Director of Sales: Neil Levin
Director of Financial Operations: J. Brian Birky

WELDON OWEN PTY LTD
Publisher: Sheena Coupe
Managing Editor: Lynn Humphries
Project Editor: Liz Connolly
Designers: Clive Collins, Clare Forte